bubblefacts...

WILD WEATHER

Miles Kelly
PUBLISHING

First published in 2005 by
Miles Kelly Publishing Ltd
Bardfield Centre, Great Bardfield, Essex, CM7 4SL

2 4 6 8 10 9 7 5 3 1

Publishing Director:
Anne Marshall

Cartoons:
Mark Davis

Editorial Assistant:
Hannah Todd

Designer:
Louisa Leitao

Senior Editor:
Belinda Gallagher

Production:
Estela Boulton

ISBN 1–84236–520–7

Printed in China

British Library Cataloguing-in-Publication Data
A catalogue record for this book is available from the British Library

Indexer: Jane Parker

www.mileskelly.net
info@mileskelly.net

Contents

Four seasons

spring to winter

Spring, summer, autumn and winter are the four seasons. Our planet plots a path around the Sun that takes a year. As Earth is tilted, first one and then the other Pole leans towards the Sun, giving us seasons. In June, for example, the North Pole leans towards the Sun, bringing summer to the northern half of the world.

G'NIGHT!

G'DAY!

I LOVE A NICE SHOWER!

MAN, THAT'S ONE CRAZY HAIRSTYLE!

WELL, AT LEAST WE HAVE SOME HAIR...

The seasons give us different kinds of weather. Summer is usually sunny and warm.

In autumn, some trees lose their leaves, but evergreens keep theirs all year round.

In winter the weather can be very cold, and there may be heavy snow showers.

Wind and rain

Monsoons are winds that carry heavy rains. These rains fall in the tropics during a hot, rainy season. The Sun warms up the sea, which causes huge banks of cloud to form. Monsoons then blow these clouds towards land. Once the rains hit the land, they can pour for weeks.

When the rains are heavy they can cause chaos, as streets turn to rivers and homes are swept away.

Many parts of the tropics have just two seasons. They are the areas closest to the Equator. Here it is always hot, as these places are constantly facing the Sun.

In parts of monsoon India, over 26,000 millimetres of rain have fallen in a single year!

Rainforests have rain all year round. Even the dry season is wet, just not as wet as the wet season!

What a scorcher!
solar power!

The Sun is a star, a super-hot ball of burning gases. It gives off heat rays that travel 150 million kilometres through space to our planet. During the journey, the rays cool down, but they are still strong and they can scorch the Earth.

MAN, THAT SAND IS HOT!

YEP, THAT'S WHAT YOU GET IN DESERTS!

GREAT BARBIE THIS IS! NO BANGERS, NO BURGERS...

SAND! NOTHING BUT SAND!

People living in the Sahara Desert cover their skin from top to toe to protect it from the Sun.

Sometimes, as sunlight passes through our atmosphere, it hits layers of air at different temperatures. This makes the air and the light bend and can trick our eyes into seeing something that is not there. This is called a mirage.

The hottest place on Earth is Al Aziziyah in Libya. It is 58°C in the shade – hot enough to fry an egg!

OOPS! HAS SOMEONE PULLED THE PLUG OUT?

SQUAWK!

ROAST RABBIT, ANYONE?

VERY FUNNY!

Too much sunshine can bring drought. When forests are very dry they can catch alight and burn rapidly.

Our atmosphere
layers of gas

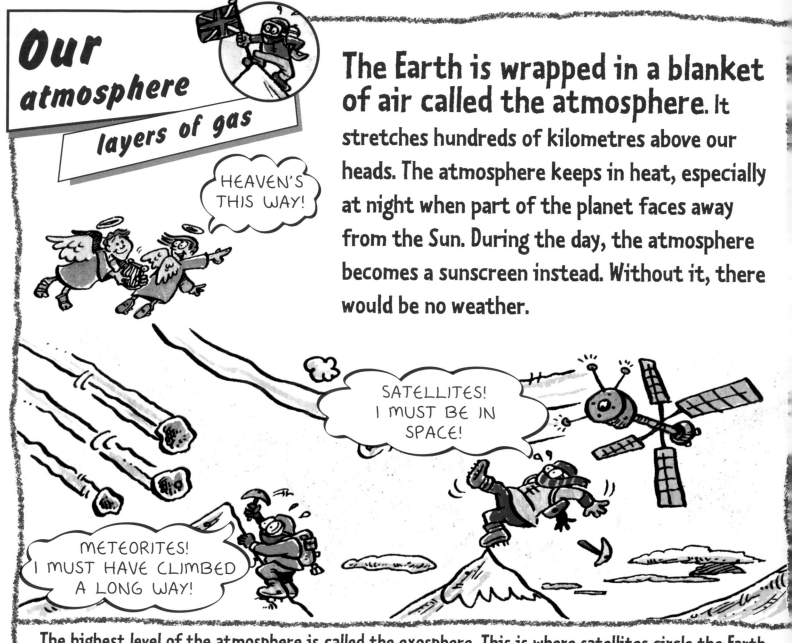

The Earth is wrapped in a blanket of air called the atmosphere. It stretches hundreds of kilometres above our heads. The atmosphere keeps in heat, especially at night when part of the planet faces away from the Sun. During the day, the atmosphere becomes a sunscreen instead. Without it, there would be no weather.

HEAVEN'S THIS WAY!

SATELLITES! I MUST BE IN SPACE!

METEORITES! I MUST HAVE CLIMBED A LONG WAY!

The highest level of the atmosphere is called the exosphere. This is where satellites circle the Earth.

Curtains of light occur in the atmosphere when light particles collide with air molecules.

Most weather occurs in the troposphere, the layer of atmosphere about 10 kilometres above your head.

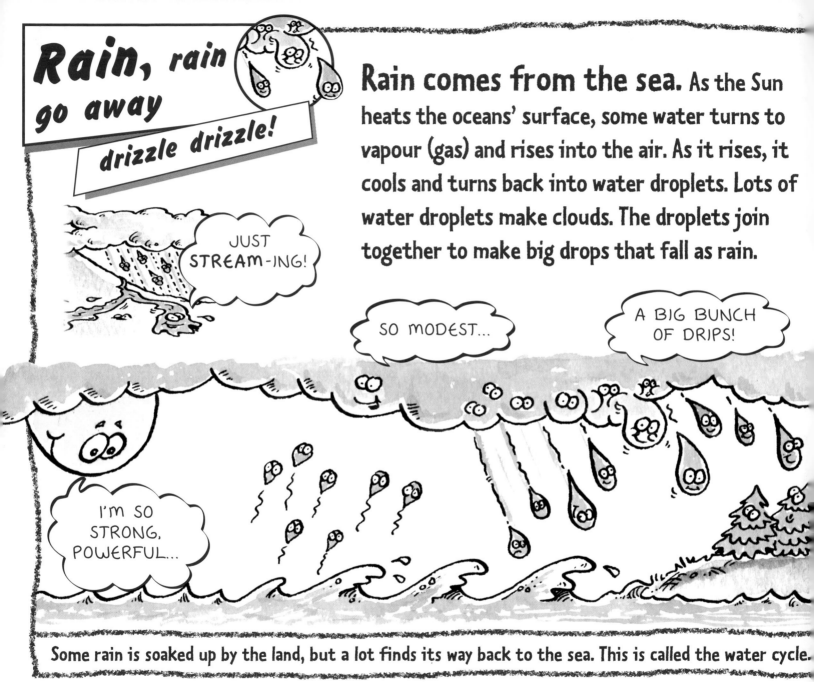

Rain, rain go away

drizzle drizzle!

Rain comes from the sea. As the Sun heats the oceans' surface, some water turns to vapour (gas) and rises into the air. As it rises, it cools and turns back into water droplets. Lots of water droplets make clouds. The droplets join together to make big drops that fall as rain.

JUST STREAM-ING!

SO MODEST...

A BIG BUNCH OF DRIPS!

I'M SO STRONG, POWERFUL...

Some rain is soaked up by the land, but a lot finds its way back to the sea. This is called the water cycle.

Some people say that cows lay down when rain is coming but there is no truth in it!

Some rain never reaches the ground. The raindrops turn back into water vapour because they hit a layer of super-dry air. You can actually see the drops falling like a curtain from the cloud, but the curtain stops in mid-air. This type of weather is called virga.

DO I LOOK LIKE I'M GROWING A BEARD?

AT LAST, A NICE COLD DRINK!

I LOVE A DROP OF RAIN!

...en moving air hits a mountain the air is forced upwards – as it travels up it cools down and clouds form.

Flood warning

waterworks!

PITTER PATTER!

Too much rain brings floods. Flash floods happen after a short burst of heavy rainfall, usually caused by thunderstorms. Broadscale flooding happens when rain falls steadily over a wide area – for weeks or months – without stopping. When this happens, rivers eventually burst their banks. Tropical storms can also lead to broadscale flooding.

WHAT A WASH-OUT.

HELP! MY ARMBANDS ARE AT HOME!

FORTY DAYS AND NIGHTS OF THIS...

When a lot of rain falls very quickly onto baked dry land it cannot soak in – so even deserts can flood.

The ancient Egyptians said the goddess Isis filled the River Nile with tears, as she cried for her lost husband.

There really was a Great Flood. The Bible tells of a terrible flood, and how a man called Noah was saved. Recently, explorers found the first real evidence of the Flood – a sunken beach 140 metres below the surface of the Black Sea. There are ruins of houses, dating back to 5600BC. Stories of a huge flood in ancient times do not appear only in the Bible – the Babylonians and Greeks told of one, too.

WHERE'S THAT DARNED DOVE GOT TO?

THERE'S NO PLEASING SOME PEOPLE!

I CAN'T BEAR HAVING MUDDY FEET!

...ud can flood! On bare mountains there are no tree roots to hold soil together, so mudslides can happen.

Deep freeze

getting chilly!

Snow is made of tiny crystals.

When air temperatures are very cold – around 0°C – the water droplets in the clouds freeze to make tiny ice crystals. Sometimes, individual crystals fall, but usually they clump together into snowflakes.

Snow is made worse by strong winds that can cause deep drifts. No two snowflakes are ever the same.

Antarctica is the coldest place on Earth. Temperatures of $-89.2°C$ have been recorded there.

Avalanches are like giant snowballs. They happen after lots of snow falls on a mountain. The slightest movement or noise can jolt the pile of snow and start it moving down the slope. As it crashes down, the avalanche picks up extra snow and can bury whole towns.

WHOOPS... DID I MISS?

LEG IT!

IT'S SUCH FUN ON THE PISTE!

IT'S SNOW JOKE!

Marksmen shoot at snowy mountains to set off avalanches. This stops too much snow from building up.

Winds of change

life's a breeze!

Wind is moving air. Winds blow because air is constantly moving from areas of high pressure to areas of low pressure. The bigger the difference in temperature between the two areas, the faster the wind blows.

Wind strength is measured using the Beaufort Scale. Force 0 is calm, while Force 12 is a hurricane.

Wind can be harnessed and used to generate electricity. It is an environmentally friendly power source.

Strong winds in southern Germany have been blamed for causing road accidents and bouts of madness!

Eye of the hurricane
on land and sea

Some winds travel at speeds of more than 120 kilometres an hour. Violent tropical storms occur when strong winds blow into an area of low pressure and start to spin very fast. They develop over warm seas and pick up speed until they reach land, where there is no more moist sea air to feed them. Such storms bring torrential rain.

BIG HEAD!

WHOOOSHHH!

WHAT A BIG EYE YOU HAVE!

DON'T BE SUCKED IN BY IT!

Hurricane hunters are planes that fly close to a storm. They take measurements that can predict its path

Tropical storms over the Atlantic are called hurricanes, while storms over the Pacific are called typhoons.

The centre of a hurricane is calm and still. This part is called the eye. As the eye of the storm passes over, there is a pause in the terrifying rains and wind. Hurricanes even have names! One of the worst hurricanes was Hurricane Andrew, which battered the coast of Florida in 1992.

In the 13th century, a terrible storm at sea prevented Genghis Khan from invading Japan!

Fluffy clouds

way up high!

Clouds come in all shapes and sizes. To help recognize them, scientists split them into ten basic types. Each type depends on what a cloud looks like and where it forms in the sky. The three main types of cloud – cirrus, cumulus and stratus – were named in the 1800s by British scientist Luke Howard.

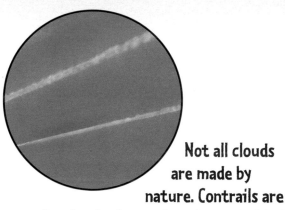

Not all clouds are made by nature. Contrails are streaky clouds that a plane leaves behind as it flies. They are made of water vapour that comes from the plane's engines. The second it hits the cold air, the vapour turns into ice crystals, leaving a trail of snow-white cloud.

Cumulus clouds bring rain

The biggest cumulus clouds, cumulus congestus, bring the heaviest rain showers.

Cirrus clouds appear at great
heights from the ground

Contrails

Cirrostratus

Cumulonimbus clouds
give heavy showers

Stratus clouds can bring drizzle
or appear as fog

Patches of cloud like shimmering fish scales are called mackerel skies. They indicate changeable weather.

Thunder and lightning

it's electrifying!

Hot weather creates warm, moist air that rises to form huge cumulonimbus clouds. Inside each cloud, water droplets and ice crystals bang about, building up electrical charges. Electricity flows between the charges, creating lightning. This is so hot, it expands the air around it, making a loud noise or thunderclap.

Sheet lightning jumps from cloud to cloud. Lightning that travels to the ground is called fork lightning.

If there's rain in a thundercloud, lightning looks red, if there's hail, it looks blue. Lightning can also be yellow or white.

Tall buildings are protected from lightning. Church steeples and other tall structures are often struck by bolts of lightning. This could damage the building, or give electric shocks to people inside, so lightning conductors are placed on the roof. These channel the lightning safely away.

BIT OF AN ICY ATMOSPHERE.

ELECTRIFYING EXPERIENCE!

OOPS!!

SQUAWK!

ZZZ!

eople do survive lightning strikes, but it is rare. Hailstones are chunks of ice, and can be as big as melons!

Weather it out!

myth or reality?

YEP, I'M ONE HOT STAR!

Seaweed can tell us if rain is on the way. Long ago, people looked to nature for clues about the weather. One traditional way of forecasting was to hang up strands of seaweed. If the seaweed remained slimy, the air was damp and rain was likely. If the seaweed shrivelled up, the weather would be dry.

Seaweed can tell us how damp the air is. A groundhog's shadow supposedly means cold weather to come!

The earliest weather records are over 3000 years old. They were scratched down onto a piece of tortoiseshell by Chinese weather watchers. The inscriptions describe when it rained, snowed and how windy it was.

Can you believe it?

Weather balloons with scientific equipment are launched each day. Their readings are radioed back to the ground.

A red sunset is supposed to be followed by a fine morning. A clear night sky means that frost is likely.

Made for weather

creature comforts

Camels can go for two weeks without any water. These animals are adapted to life in a hot, dry climate. They do not sweat until their body temperature hits 40°C, which helps them to save water. The humps on their backs store fat, which is used for energy when food and water are scarce.

The spadefoot toad lives underground in the desert. Lizards such as geckos also live in hot, dry areas.

Polar bears live in freezing conditions. Beneath their gleaming white fur they have black skin. This helps them to soak up as much warmth as possible from the Sun.

Acorn woodpeckers turn tree trunks into larders. In autumn, when acorns are ripe, the birds collect as many as they can.

IT'S RUDE TO STICK YOUR TONGUE OUT!

CHILL OUT, BRO!

OI! TEA LEAF!

Polar bears have thick fur and plenty of body fat to keep them warm. Squirrels store nuts for winter.

Weather watch
tools of the trade

The first known weather station was built around 75BC in Athens, Greece. The Tower of Winds was an eight-sided building. It had a wind vane on the roof and a water clock inside.

The Tower of Winds was built by Andronicus of Cyrrhus. Weather cocks show the direction of the wind.

Barometers measure air pressure. The first barometer was made by an Italian student in 1643.

Weather house figures detect moisture in the air. Fahrenheit invented the thermometer in 1714.

Index